T0207602

At Peace

Healing God's Way

KIM PHILLIPS

© 2022 Kim Phillips. All rights reserved.

No part of this book may be reproduced, stored in a retrieval system, or
transmitted by any means without the written permission of the author.

AuthorHouse™
1663 Liberty Drive
Bloomington, IN 47403
www.authorhouse.com
Phone: 833-262-8899

Because of the dynamic nature of the Internet, any web addresses or links contained in this book may have changed
since publication and may no longer be valid. The views expressed in this work are solely those of the author and do
not necessarily reflect the views of the publisher, and the publisher hereby disclaims any responsibility for them.

Any people depicted in stock imagery provided by Getty Images are models,
and such images are being used for illustrative purposes only.
Certain stock imagery © Getty Images.

Scripture quotations are from the Holy Bible, King James Version (Authorized Version). First published in 1611.
Quoted from the KJV Classic Reference Bible, Copyright © 1983 by The Zondervan Corporation.

Scripture quotations are taken from the Holy Bible, New International Version®, NIV®.
Copyright © 1973, 1978, 1984 by Biblica, Inc.™
Used by permission of Zondervan. All rights reserved worldwide.

Interior illustrations Brittany Huntley.

This book is printed on acid-free paper.

ISBN: 978-1-6655-6459-5 (sc)
ISBN: 978-1-6655-6458-8 (e)

Library of Congress Control Number: 2022912767

Print information available on the last page.

Published by AuthorHouse 10/13/2022

authorHOUSE®

CONTENTS

PROLOGUE

With the pandemic going on and not knowing where to turn, let me assure you, first, you are strong enough to withstand anything that comes your way with the right focus and mindset. Secondly, you are loved and favored by the Almighty. There are some people who never experience life fully because of their past. I want to tell you to do the opposite. Because of your past, live life to the fullest. Sometimes we are left wondering whatever happened to the good or peace that we search for in life.

Well, my friend, I want you to know it is still there. Just like a soft wind that blows with the sweet fragrance of a beautiful unknown flower, it is there to delight your senses and cause you to search for it. After you have searched a while, you find it. That is how peace can come upon you, or you can lose it. because you have not sought after it.

When we talk about peace, many ideas, pictures, or cozy thoughts come to mind. A love from long ago, maybe a family member that supported your wild and crazy ideas, or a pet that made you feel wanted and special. Like you can take on the world and win.

Then reality takes a bite out of it. Lost love. Dionne Warwick sang a song, "Finders of Lost Love" (telling my age here), but when you listen to the lyrics, it required us to find that love outside of ourselves. Only to be dissatisfied with who we are and stay on the hamster wheel. Trust me, the decades of searching for someone outside of oneself to be happy can be a full-time job. Only to become disenchanted with life.

To be genuinely happy, you must first recognize what happy looks like, and that must start in you. Then, can you recognize happiness when it comes? You will not jump from relationship to relationship or place to place because you will realize joy, peace, and happiness starts and ends with you fulfilling your destiny.

Sometimes we negate to do the necessary things to get where we want to be. Meaning we look at people and things and go after them, not recognizing the road or struggle the person has endured to get to that place. We accept counterfeit behavior, things, and lifestyles to appear to have achieved a particular status. It will come back to haunt you. Your peace ought to be more valuable than what things look like to others. I get it; we hear everyone is doing it. Really, can we honestly say everyone is doing something? That, my friend, is a hasty generalization. We do not know, but your personal peace should matter more to you than what others appear to be doing.

Let me tell you a story. It will not be brief or pretty, although true. And then, you can decide whether to continue to follow the path of someone else instead of who you were created to be. My personal story will hopefully inspire you to recognize that if I had the strength to do it, so do you. Again, I am sharing in the hopes of motivating you to look at things in a different light and strengthen you by letting you see that real starts within you and then sheds outside.

You cannot contain something so powerful that it attracts the best and sometimes brings ole slew foot him/her to you. I began this journey of peace after having what I will describe as a horrific childhood, and while some may disagree, that is their prerogative. We must face our life head on and live our best, blessed life.

Today some of the things that were hidden or not openly discussed are now being exposed for the hideous things that they are. I am profoundly grateful that there are adults that stand up for children and continue to protect them. I am purposefully living life with my family. It is a choice that I have chosen, and regardless of how many times my mind wanders back to my childhood, I continue to thank God and talk about it with my husband. So, here is what I promised. I know you may know someone who has shared the story before or you may have a similar story. I would encourage you to rewrite how it will impact your future self to be happy and find your peace.

1

CHAPTER

School Days

My life started in kindergarten. These are the first memories that I had of school. My teacher, Ms. Z and her sister were old and walked slow. To a child, every adult walks slow, and we were impatient to get outside and play. We had recess and snack time after lunch. What in the world was the school thinking? Anyway, we had a regular schedule for activities. One of them included having the local bank come to our school for the children to open a bank account and have the dentist look at our teeth.

Of course, you could not have an account without your parents' permission. So, the notices were given to everyone. I tell you, that was one of the funniest things that happened at five years old. Coming home from school and telling your mom or dad you had a note for them. Usually, when a note was sent home with the child, it was attached with a big safety pin to the chest, and we were not the most delicate people on the planet.

Running around in the playground until someone older came to escort you home. What a laugh; they would be the one to read it first, and then it would get to the parent. Obviously, that did not work for most of us. So, they would write it inside our notebook to be signed by the parent. I believe that system worked better. Mom gave her consent , and every Wednesday and Friday, like clockwork, the bank came to collect whatever we were given. We received a bank book. Hopefully, the photo resonates with some of you.

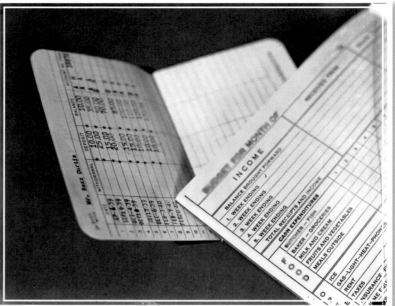

In the 60s, this is what the bank gave to everyone with an account. Getting permission to open a bank account was the highlight of kindergarten. Big times ahead. The schools back in those days taught more than socialization. They were interested in helping the student become a productive citizen (I guess). It felt good knowing that we were doing something so grown-up. Every Saturday, my younger sister and I would go to the bank with my mother and watch her put money in the bank or withdraw money. Either way, we knew it was something we wanted to do when we grew up.

She would say, save and do not spend. What kind of madness was that? We would compare how much money we had in our account with our friends, and that is when everything went off the rails. It became a competition to save more than the others. Cute for kids, not for adults (just saying).

I do not recall the first or second grade. I can tell you that most of my classmates were assigned to the same teacher every year. I still cannot quite understand that, but we were. We knew at the end of the school year when we compared report cards who was going to what teacher and class. And that group stayed together unless you transferred to another school. Now the third grade, boy, that was when things started going south in a big way. Going in and out of the building meant holding hands with the opposite sex or fighting to hold hands with your bestie. Either way, it was controlled chaos in the hallways for the teachers every time we would line up to leave the room.

Ms. B was our teacher. She was nice most of the time. We would push and trip one another in the hallway or scream and watch the teacher get flustered. Then the whole class would have to write 100 times I will not misbehave and have our parents sign it. It was fun.

During those times, teachers would call or pop up at your house without telling you why. Imagine the look on our faces when the teacher came knocking on your door just before dinner time. And you did not answer the door if an adult was in the house.

Hence, "my parents are not home" would not work. You would sit ever so politely while they discussed your behavior in class and not interrupt. For those of you who never had a teacher come knock on your door, lucky you. Although, most of the time, it was because of my brothers acting up in the hallways.

In those days, every student had to read out loud. The teacher would go around the classroom and one by one call out your name, you were supposed to pick up reading where the last person stopped. Well, they also told you to sound out the word if you did not know it. Of course, when it came to me, the word island came up, so I said is-land. She did not tell me to put it back together again, and of course, I found myself writing on the blackboard 100 times I will not disrupt class.

All my friends were laughing, but those when she recognized their voices had to write on the other side of the board I will not make fun of anyone in class. Penmanship was paramount to your success too. Like they knew everything that would happen before it happened. If you were too rambunctious, you found your seat in front of the class next to the teacher. We had to write in cursive. And before we were able to leave at the end of the day, wash the board off. We had the big black erasers and chalk. We were doing the janitor's job and not getting paid. I had a friend whom, it never seemed to fail, missed having to read out loud.

That is probably why she did not get in trouble as much. Like clockwork, she was excused from class to go to religious instructions. I tell you, that was the perfect excuse for her every week. It was only for the Catholics in the school, but she also had an older sister in the school that did not go. And, one week, they were calling out the names for them to line up, and she was not on the list. Little miss stowaway was ratted out by her older sister. I laughed. Well, to tell the truth, the whole class laughed, and everyone was held over after school.

Can you imagine at minimum 28 children being in detention? Our parents or whoever was picking us up had to come upstairs to the class and get us. Looking back on that, it was a shame. The teacher had to stay late, and that meant messing up her plans for the evening as well.

Every Friday, we had assembly. We had to wear blue jumpers and white blouses. The boys had navy blue pants and white shirts with ties. As part of the chorus group, we would sing the school motto:

We go to P.S. 54, where each day we learn more and more. Learning and playing makes our friendships grow, character above all is our motto, reading, writing and penmanship, science, music, and arithmetic, with the help of books you can open any door, do your best on the tests at P.S. 54, where each day we learn more and more.

I remember one day, she did not show up. The principal had to come get us from the cafeteria and take us to our classroom. The substitute teacher was an old lady with glasses who didn't look friendly at all. The principal announced our regular teacher would not be returning for a while. I was mad. This was the only teacher I liked. And why did she get to stay home, and we had to go to school even when we said we were sick. The nerve of her staying home. Later we found out it was the flu, how? Because most of us caught it. Here I was telling people I was allergic to the teacher.

When she finally came back, she was pregnant. Big and round. And yes, the class clown joked on her (behind her back of course). When I think about those days, I can hear the boys saying, yeah, she was sick, alright. Amid everything else that was going on, there was still time to laugh and act normal. As time passed, friends started moving away, we moved away, and things started to change. Connections were being lost with people you thought would be there for the rest of your life, who were are suddenly not.

Summer break was coming up. But, before the students were released for summer, the doctor or nurse in the school would give you a shot. I do not know what it was, but every student received it. Vaccinations were provided with or without the consent of the parent.

How dare they give me a shot? Anyway, I took the shot like a champ. I do not recall how long it was before I became deathly ill. There was no way after school was out to find out what type of vaccination was given. So, I found myself seriously sick. It was so bad that the church went on a fast for my healing. Here I must give glory and praise to God and thank my siblings for their faith being strong enough.

I could not walk far, run, eat, or play without throwing up. My eyes turned yellow and became jaundiced. My mother did not know what to do. Every day for weeks, I would be at the county hospital being examined. I could not be in a hot room or in light.

We had to ride the bus home from the hospital, and when the bus was crowded, I would overheat and had to get off the bus. It was a long ride home. We stopped at the store along the way to get water. It did not stay down. So, my mom resorted to ice pops to keep me hydrated.

When we finally reached home, my mother called my siblings in and gave them the medical report. It was grim. My sisters and brothers started crying and hugging all over me. Pull yourself together, people. I honestly did not know how sick I was.

The doctor told my mother that I would not make it with the way my body was reacting to the vaccination. I had to stay out of the sun and was bedridden because I was too weak to walk far, and my breathing was laborious.

This is where my faith began. And as I started to believe in God, a wonderful woman I met during camping became ill. She lived in another state, and her sisters called for the church to pray and fast for her healing. Time stood still for that moment. My healing and trust became paramount for someone else's healing. I prayed, please God heal her. If you do, I will really serve you.

Well, she pulled through surgery, and I accepted Christ as my savior. I felt like God proved to me that day, but I did not know the road I had to walk. Sometimes we must forget about our moment (s) of despair and pray for someone else. You never know who is praying for you.

While all this was going on, my birthday came I am still outliving the verdict of the doctor! I turned nine. With everything that transpired, my brothers convinced me to ask our mom for a bicycle for my birthday. Since it was in August, I figured what the heck. After going through such an ordeal, who would deny me?

My brothers said they would teach me how to ride it, and I would be the coolest girl on the block. They lied. It was so they could take it and ride up and down with their friends. Just in case you did not know, I got the bike.

Getting a bike was an important thing for us. I bragged about it to my friends or anybody who would listen. The boys on the block would say girls do not ride bikes. I was a tomboy, so that did not apply to me. There was this Italian guy on the block. A brother from another mother kind of thing. He hung out with my brothers, which the family referred to as the three musketeers for some reason. Anyway, when I told him, he said he would teach me how to ride it. When I finally got the bike, it was an orange, no speed bike. The one with no gears and the brakes are in the pedal.

This is what the bike looked like, except it was orange. So do not judge me; my mom got it for my birthday. And I probably rode it until I got tired of fighting my brother for it.

During the summer, my brothers would borrow my bike to go to the store to get lunch for us. There was this store called Perez'. You could go there and get a hero sandwich (which today is called a sub) and pay $1.50 to $2.00 depending on what you wanted on it. Most of the time, we would get spiced ham, American cheese, lettuce, tomato, and mayonnaise. If we wanted to get fancy, add extra meat or cheese for a little bit more. My brothers would take my bike and say they were coming straight back. They never did. After they ate their lunch, they would wind up playing basketball at the park with their friends and come home with some wild story about losing the money or flat out say they forgot.

The excuse was, they could not come back fast unless they rode my bike. So, I let them. They had all kinds of stories ready to tell us. So, when I got tired, I went to my other brother's (the Italian one) house and told him. He promised to teach me how to ride my bike. And he did. He stopped my brothers from taking it from me. Of course, I could not go to the store to get the sandwiches because it meant leaving the neighborhood riding alone, and I could not. So, from that moment on we, my younger sister and I, began to plot how to get our lunch and make sure our brothers did not spend our money.

I do not recall how that went after that. Let it suffice to say, we started getting even with them every time we did not get our food. I was the first of my mother's children to get a bicycle.

Every year like clockwork my best friend would give me a pure white puppy for my birthday. We would name the dog Snowball. We were so focused on the puppy that the bicycle became a thing of the past. And like clockwork, my middle brother would always think this puppy had special powers. Unlike the other dogs. This one could fly.

So, the professor, aka middle brother, would put a mattress in the backyard, go to the roof, and toss the puppy down. Each time, the puppy would bounce on top of the mattress and stay. Until one day, my sister and I climbed onto the roof and saw what he was doing. I showed him puppies do not fly, and neither did he. Yes, if you thought I pushed him, I did. He landed on the mattress, too.

I told you that to help you see that in everything, there is joy. He stopped. I finally had a puppy who survived the mattress. Summer was over and school was starting again.

School was in session for the fall, and that is where the stuff hit the fan.

We lived in a big house. Three floors. Where one of the older sisters lived in the basement with her children, we were sandwiched in between on the main floor, and another sister lived upstairs. It was fun in that house. We played all kinds of games and had to sleep with at least six to eight people in the same bed. Sometimes we raced to bed to make sure we had a place to sleep. The fortunate ones were able to sleep under the window to have air blowing over the stink feet of the person at the bottom of the bed.

All the girls were in one bed, and our brothers had bunk beds on the other side of the room. Oh yeah, mom had a lot of children. There were fourteen children. Since the writing of this book, my youngest brother and two of my sisters are deceased. And we have nieces and nephews that are older than us. Think about that.

We all lived together at one time or another growing up. The girls played hairdressers, and the boys did whatever they do. One day, we were playing in the basement of the house like we were at the beautician and my niece cut my hair. We were supposed to be pretending, but an enormous chunk of my hair was cut out of the middle of my head. That was the scariest day of all our lives. Were we mischievous? I will let you decide. We had fun. I had to have all my hair cut off by a barber, and that is when my sister moved out.

We had an older sister who lived in the basement apartment. She was washing clothes, and we were jumping up and down above her head. She kept hollering for us to go outside and play. In the meantime, she was wringing out her clothes and got her hand stuck in the wringer. This is similar to what the machine looked like. We had to hang the clothes on a line in the backyard to dry.

I know how she got her hand stuck in the wringer, because you had to push the clothes through to get the water out. I guess she was so busy yelling at us to realize what was going on. Our oldest sister was home she worked in the hospital. She heard her screaming and helped get her hand out of the wringer. We got a whipping for that too. We had so many of those until we created a sheet of who got the most beatings for something they did or did not do. In those days, if you were around, you got it. I guess they figured you were guilty, too.

By this time, school was about to start again. It meant we would have to do homework and go to bed at a decent time. Where did the time go? I wanted to discuss the brevity of summer with the establishment and let them know I was not satisfied with their decision. Anyway, school started, and by this time some of my sisters moved away. We moved out of the house as well.

We moved to Brownsville. A few of our siblings moved close by. We had nephews and nieces that came to visit. So, the world was right again. My sister and I had to ride the public bus to school until we transferred to a local school. We moved far enough from the church that I figured we would not have to go anymore. What was I thinking? By the end of school, we were back in the old neighborhood. Close to the mess that caused families to fight and break covenant with each other. I guess she had to get us back into the house of the Lord before we really got out of hand. So, back into the neighborhood where all our old friends lived. And the fights began.

Let me tell you, with all those shenanigans, every Easter weekend without fail, my mother would send us to the beauty parlor to get our hair straightened and curled. Boy, Ms. Fields had all the girls on the block's hair looking good. She would burn the top of our ears with the straightening comb if we moved. She would say, now I am going near your ear; hold it and be still, so I do not burn you. Wait, you are supposed to be a professional, right? How could you burn my ears? Sometimes she did, and sometimes she did not; I guess it comes with the territory or a part of beauty. Now, we have perms. Burning the scalp is rough.

When she was finished, our mom would come pick us up and walk us home. We could not touch our hair and had to wrap it up at night. Taking a bath was hard because we could not get our hair wet, so we would put plastic bags on our heads and dive underwater. Take that, lady! I guess the last laugh was on us. We still went to church; just the edges of our hair would curl up.

Dressed in white from head to toe, pocketbook, gloves, and shoes (the saints went marching in). Our brothers had on suit and tie with dress shoes. Because they were not thoroughly checked, they would put on tube socks, and they were able to get away with it. Looking like little ushers, how awful. But I guess mom liked it, and that was all that mattered.

This Sunday changed my life forever. My mother took us to church like a proud peacock. We walked past some of the same kids we would fight with every day, and of course, they would clown us about being dressed up. On this Easter Sunday, 1969, however, the five of us, three youngest boys and the girls, had to go with mom to church. What was her problem? We believed in God (I guess). I do not know about them, but I wavered in my belief. We did not take His name in vain, so what was her problem?

Anyway, we walked about three blocks to this big church. It used to be a Jewish synagogue. It had a lot of stairs, but it was nice. Anyway, when we finally got in, they were singing and clapping their hands. The music was on point. However, what she did after that haunted us for years to come. They invited people to join. My proud peacock took all of us up front and gave them our names and ages. Why? Why did you do that? I was not consulted on that at all. Next thing we knew, everybody was shaking our hands and hugging us. Why? Because Ms. PP (proud peacock), aka mom, signed us up to become members of the church. We looked at each other, and I guess what was going through our minds was, huh.

On our way home from church, we did not feel different or act different. There were children on our block who did not go church and teased us. They got away with it that Sunday. Our siblings did not send their children to church. Why us? I guess we needed to be somewhere besides in the basement or backyard, killing one another. The next week when we went to church with white shoes and pocketbooks, one of our friends started teasing us.

That did not bode well for him. Suffice it to say, when parents gave children money and sent them to church, they were supposed to give instructions with it. We saved it for candy on the way home. My sister and I chased him around the parked cars and hit him in the head with a pocketbook full of candy and coins. He had to get stitches for that, but he did not earn his lesson. We did not know any better, better; I guess neither did he.

Soon after, they began picking us up for church services. My mom did not let us go during the weekly services on Wednesdays and Fridays. But Sundays, we belonged to them. We joined the Sunshine band, which was that was the name of the children's choir. Although, I will speak for myself, I did not want any part of the whole shenanigans.

I cannot begin to tell you half of the mess that began to happen. Once we were members, things and people on the block began to change. I guess back then, when you were a single mom, the best or only place people turned was the church. There were a lot of single mothers around and kids to play with. Heck, some of them went to the same school, so you were comfortable being there. But the secrets within are what change a person's life forever.

As fall approached, our attendance at church began to slow down. My mom worked two jobs. One was at the hospital and the other was at a chocolate candy factory during the holiday season. During that time, she would bring home a box of chocolates for all of us. And it would be around Christmas time, when she would really rack up on the sweets. On her days off work, she would start baking cakes and cooking for the holidays.

For Christmas, like clockwork, the boys would get underwear and socks and the girls received toys. We got an Easy-Bake Oven. We were not allowed to use it without parental supervision, of course we did. Our brothers were supposed to be our lookout guys to make sure mom did not catch us using it. You could not tell us we were not cooking like her. We would use the leftovers and bake cakes with the mix that came with it. We were hot stuff.

Well, we did that so often until our spies forgot to watch out for mom coming home. We had to pull the cord out of the wall to keep the house from smelling like we used the oven. I guess they were so busy playing cops and robbers until they forgot the saloon was being run by underage owners. We got in big trouble because you could smell the food when you entered the house.

For some reason unbeknownst to us (the children), we had to move. Our Easy-Bake was stolen. So for Christmas as usual, we got another kitchen item (was she trying to tell us something?). This one looked like a little stove, and as usual, we put food in it again. But this time, one of my brothers got burnt trying to open it. That one looked like a mini oven, and a bell would ding when the cake was done.

Easy-Bake Oven-illustration by Brittany Huntley

I guess we should been in church ha ha. But, if I recall correctly, we had one sister living upstairs , and she said anything, except I am going to tell mommy. What? Don't you have your child to tend to? We were put on punishment because the boys copped out on us. Our punishment meant we could not play with the oven anymore. As a result, you got to hear this, we started fighting or at least I did with our older brothers. Now the middle one is and was my favorite. Something is wrong with that man; I just have not told him yet.

While we were on punishment, we had to stay on the main floor, which is where we lived. There was a ceiling light fixture; it had a medallion and bulb outlets surrounding the edges. This is the closest I could find to give you a visual of what the ceiling in the house looked like. The bulbs went around the base of the fixture, so one could change the bulbs when they would blow out. The web can be a wonderful thing. Now, I need you to imagine, around the interior of the fixture four bulbs are placed there. Well, remove one because it blew and was not replaced, so the outlet was empty. Anyway, my middle brother was making me upset about something.

How we had that in the house, one will never know. We still ask where it came from. The picture was provided by Black Rock Galleries. I do not recall bringing it home, but it was useful. Now, picture it in your mind... arguing with your sibling, and that pole is sitting there all lonely. I talked him into sticking it in the socket while I stood near the switch.

I know what you are thinking... at first, I did not touch the button. I let him stick the pole in it without powering it. I told him do it again. This time I really did push the power button. Yes, he got shocked and dropped the pole, and I told him he had white blood; he was from out of space. See, kids can be cruel. He ran around in a circle until I calmed him down and had him do it again. I did not touch the switch the last time, but I shocked him twice because he hit me. I tell you, older siblings should not really mess with the young ones. We will get you back.

Moving forward from that moment, we were probably the closest siblings. I told him no one will ever hurt him again. I will get them for him. It is odd how women and men view things in life. I would go with him to his teacher's house because she wanted to tutor him. I told him that was not right. He was fed the line about not be held back in school because he could not do the work.

After a few times going to the teacher's house, I asked him why they were in the room instead of in the kitchen where I sat waiting. This did not sit well with me, but I did not know who to talk to. So, every time he went to her house, I trailed along. She was not going to pull the wool over my eyes. Parents, sisters, brothers, aunty, or uncle, if the child says the teacher wants to meet with them alone, make it your business or someone's business to be there. Although my brother enjoyed the time spent with her, I did not think it was right for her to do that.

And we moved. We left that house and moved to another house across the street near the corner. I do not know why. As a child, you do not think much about where you live or what your parents provided for you back then. We lived in obliviousness as far as knowing what our parents were going through. All we knew as children, the adults provided shelter, food, and clothing.

We were kept ignorant of the intricacies of adulthood and what it took for our parents to make ends meet. There would be times when I recall our not eating dinner at all. Maybe she was tired or there was not enough to go around. Welfare provided can meat, block cheese, powder milk, and peanut butter. If you ever get a chance to look at the movie *Claudine* with James Earl Jones and Diahann Carroll, you would know what I mean.

Almost everybody in the neighborhood was getting food from the government. There was a song about the cheese, but it made a mean grilled cheese sandwich; I know that much. Whether we had enough food did not cross our minds, we just went along our merry way. I look back now and am totally grateful in a way. The weight of having to provide for your family is great.

When things started getting a little rough because mom started working for the hospital, we were cut off from welfare. Oh yeah, they came by to check up on who lived in the house, just like in the movie. By that time, mom was getting paid very well but was not home to take care of us. So, she sent me and my younger sister to live with our older sister and her family. When our abuser found out, he had people coming around looking for us. My older sister did not play that. She called the police and sent us back to my mother because she worked at night as well.

We moved back and met a family who lived across the street in an apartment building on our block that we would hang out with. The girls were significantly older than us, so I guess we were like their little sisters. Anyway, they loved to sing. They had beautiful voices, and one of them used to sing to us until we got sleepy. I remember the song: In the Jungle. If we did fall asleep on the steps, they would wake us up and escort us home. They protected us from the abuser.

We looked forward to singing with them and started learning how to harmonize with each other to enter the Apollo talent show. Boy oh boy, after a few weeks of singing and spinning around, switching places with each other, and staying on key, we were ready.

Here comes the broken heart. Their mother had a heart attack. There was a lot of crying and snotty noses to go around for days. Before we could audition, their father packed up, and they moved to Georgia. We did not get to perform, but as a tribute, we continued to rehearse and promise each other we would stay in touch. That did not happen. And because of this, I am selective of the language I use when it comes to staying close.

Soon after, the molesting started again. More demanding than ever. I was a little older by that time, around 11 or 12. By this time, I believe more girls were being sacrificed to whet his appetite. For some reason or what it seemed like to me, the girls in my family were continuously sought by him.

I told you about my sister. She told me she hid herself so he could not touch her. She also sacrificed herself to keep him from touching us, to no avail. When I told her I was writing the book she said, "Good, it needs to be told what happened." And she did not care who liked it or not. It is the truth. She became pregnant by him at 14 and had the baby. Things changed and she is a wonderful mother to all her children, but she wanted the world to know her life was changed forever. I mention her here because the pain of being taken advantage of sexually can and does happen everywhere. Healing is needed for everyone.

The day will come, but until then, you must find peace within yourself and move forward. I need you to know, it was not the body of Christ, aka, church but the leaders who abused their position. My sister hid in the attic, drinking to avoid him. Maybe we should have taken a page out of her book on avoidance. I did not realize she was being hurt as well. We recently had a conversation about the past and how she felt. At sixty-five, she was still carrying the wounds of childhood. Please pray for her.

By that time, I honestly stopped thinking about God. He, being God was not given a second thought. To tell the truth, I asked did He even exist. Sometimes things can become so intense that you begin to wonder if God does exist. I am not here to throw stones at anyone for their belief. What I am saying is that was one of my pet peeves about God. Why did you not rescue us? If you were so knowledgeable about everything that was going on. Where were you? Let it suffice to say, I went on a God strike. Sometimes we ask questions, and the answers come later in life or at that moment.

However, I am so glad I was not put in the position of Job. As he lamented to God about his life, he got an extraordinarily strong answer in **Job 38:1-3 Then the Lord answered Job out of the whirlwind and said, 2"Who is this that darkens counsel [questioning my authority and wisdom] By words without knowledge? 3Now gird up your loins like a man, And I will ask you, and you instruct Me!"**

Who are you that talks without knowledge? Prepare to answer with your smart self. Because I have some questions for you since you know it all. Where were you when the foundations of the earth were created? Tell me, oh knowledgeable one, how did things come into existence? Read it for yourself. I believe we will come to the same conclusion as Job; I uttered things too great for my little mind to comprehend. I apologize.

Ergo, I opened my mouth about something I could not explain if I tried. Have you ever had moments like that? Of course, if we are being real about it, we have. Thank God for His wisdom (reference to God) and mercy. Next time just ponder the thought.

After reading that scenario concerning Job, I got an answer. God said, "I sent my son to die for him, too."

Choice, my friend, is a wonderful thing. See, everyone has decision-making faculties, whether they choose to use it for good or bad is not the answer. Only knowing that you will answer one day for the things you have done ought to keep you focused on doing the right thing.

My transition to junior high did not fare that well, either. I suppose when you live within a certain radius, everyone goes to the same school. So, if you guessed, all the young people went to the same middle school. The trauma there was dramatic. At lunchtime, the entire school would be in the yard playing. It would be easy for someone to enter the yard and take a child without being noticed. The school was close to homes and the corner. One could walk up and have their pick.

So, I played near the doors where we had to line up to go back to class. In those days, you could not say whether you wanted to play outside or not. Everyone had to go outside. Getting out of school at the end of the day was a different story altogether.

Once you were let out of the building at the end of the day, you could not get back in. The doors were locked, and only the office staff was in there. If you just had to get back in, you had to stick paper in the lock to keep it from shutting. The front of the school meant you had to walk around the corner, and there you would be met by the principal asking questions. I do not remember how many times I had to fake needing to go to the bathroom to wait for him, or anyone he sent, to leave the premises. When I look back, that was probably the worst thing because it would be easier to snatch me.

Folks, I tell you, this was not how life was supposed to be at all.

Instead of enjoying childhood, you had to be careful where you went. Suspicious of everyone around you and running and hiding. Trust me, that is no way to live. I know there are many people who can identify openly or secretively; they, too, lived this kind of childhood. To you, I say I am so glad you survived. To those who have family members, friends, or know someone going through similar situations, I will ask you to keep a lookout for them.

Fear will drive some people to do drastic things that cannot be undone. I was snatched and beaten for trying to hide and there was no one around who could or would help me. Then, one of the most tragic things in my life happened. My only aunt died. If my world were messed up, then just imagine the loss of the only person I could turn to. It was devastating to put it mildly. For my graduation, she took me, my youngest sister and mom out to eat. She traveled all the way from East New York to Brooklyn just to take us out. I remember her telling my mom that she did not have to try to raise us alone. She would help. She asked what I wanted for graduation, and I said flowers and roller skates. That is truly the epitome of small thinking.

See, my aunt was single too. Her husband died before I met him. I did not want anything but to be loved. She asked my sister what she wanted, and she said for her to come to her graduation. But before her graduation, our aunt passed away. We did not know she was sick. It broke my sister's heart terribly. By the time any of the children knew she had cancer, she was dying. I believe from that moment on, my sister and I began to shut down our emotions.

A word of wisdom here... stay focused and pliable whenever possible because you will never know who God is sending to heal you. Of course, we both graduated and moved on to high school. One would think with everything that has transpired in my life, I would be a bitter old goat, ha. I began to pray and ask God for direction in life. Because if you cannot kill yourself, there must be something about you that the enemy cannot handle. That is why I am sitting here sharing with you about life and how God already plans your destiny. He will not allow you to be plucked from His hand.

King James St. John 10: 27-28

(27)"My sheep hear my voice, and I know them, and they follow me (28) and I give them eternal life; and they shall never perish, neither shall any man pluck them out of my hand."

High school was a doozy. I will keep this brief for ya... lol.

2
CHAPTER

High School Days

By that time, all the young people were going to different schools. Some stayed close to home, if possible; others were sent to what was called zoned schools. Then there were a few of us that passed exams to attend specialized schools. I was one of them. Here I guess you would probably say, did you still believe in God? The answer was yes and no. It can be complicated. Let me elucidate for you on that question. If you remember, just a minute ago, the word says, my sheep know my voice. I knew the voice of God, and oftimes, I would argue back and forth because I have a relationship with Him. So, the answer is yes, I still believed in God doing something one day that would change my life circumstances. And I trusted that intervention would come again for us. See, by this time, I was not only worried about myself but others as well. The scripture Ecclesiastes would somehow console me.

King James Version

(9) "The thing that hath been, it is that which shall be and that which is done is that which shall be done: and there is no new thing under the sun." (Ecclesiastes 1:9)

People have been doing hideous things for centuries. It did not happen to you only. There are many people that can sing this song, and some who have family members singing wish I would have stepped in. Or, in some cases, I did not know. Remember, there is nothing new going on in the world, and the future is not completely written, so we can write it for the better. Back to high school, shall we?

We moved to another borough. If you need therapy, get it. It is okay. I did. In high school because, yes, the abuser followed me through to high school. I spoke to a counselor; she sent me to a psychologist, which helped for a moment, but it did nothing about the thoughts of suicide. I wondered would God forgive me for killing myself. It gets hard when things get rough.

Some nights I cried because I remember how angry I was that no one would stop this behavior. There were plenty of girls that went in and out, and everybody on the street knew what was going on but would not say anything. Again, I did not know whether to laugh or cry because mothers would tell their sons not to get involved with any of the girls the abuser wanted. How could you?

The fear was real, and they could not or would not do anything about it. I realize some people say most of their hurt came from church, and I would agree. Where can you go when the church, which should be a place of safety, causes such irreparable harm? To God.

Today I am a minister, yes, I had to get past the church abuse and recognize that it was and is not the church. It is those who hide in them. Catholic, Protestant, Episcopal and any other denomination. The shortcomings do not belong to God; they belong to those using the template to hide their dark side. And honestly, I cannot say they did not know better because life is about choices. Whatever you decide, it is your choice, and you will have to answer for it.

The vessel is always made to perfection by its creator. Think about the paintings of Van Gogh, Warhol, Cézanne, Monet, and the list goes on. But you cannot say one of them created a painting that would be able to change its purpose. Because it could not. Neither does any animal change its nature or purpose.

Only man has been given the mind and will do as he pleases. The things we, you, have gone through are because of choice. Yes, you can stop here, cry, pray, or contemplate your life, but please, I implore you to continue reading because I promise you there are nuggets in this book that will help you move forward.

Returning to the journey, not too long starting high school I had to again become creative in getting back and forth without issue. I had friends that would ride with me and then go home, but I could not in good conscience continue to jeopardize their lives. I did not want them to get hurt trying to keep me safe. I dropped out of high school and pursued my GED. It became too stressful for me to continue hiding and trying to keep my friends from being hurt. I completed the coursework to get my GED and soon applied for college. I recall living in a four-story walk-up at the time, and he threatened to shoot me with a shotgun. He threw me down the stairs trying to kill me. Again, there were people looking at this and *screaming, "Lord, no!* but did nothing to stop him. When I got up, I shook it off and told him to shoot. I did not care anymore.

And in the midst of all this going on, I still prayed for deliverance from my abuser and had to wait on God. I did find myself praying or asking God to finish him off (for real). I prayed for his death almost as much as I prayed for mine. One way or another, it had to end. Finally, it did. He died. I was overwhelmed. I did not know how to process the final day.

Sometimes you pray for something and, when it happens, it befuddles you. I was free from the bondage, and so were many others. Here I would admonish you not to gloat because that is a soul. Yes, I was happy, yet I did not know how to live without being afraid. I did not know who I was.

After his death, we went back to live with mom in the projects. One evening as I was praying and crying asking God how to live now that I was free, a familiar spirit tried to get me to commit suicide. We were living on the 8th floor of the project. I knew it was a familiar spirit because it floated in mid-air. It looked just like him. It called me to the window and told me to jump. I remember the tv was on a gospel program. I fell on my knees and began to cry out to God. The image disappeared. I got on the phone and called the one person I knew could and would pray in a heartbeat. Her words to me were, that is a familiar spirit trying to take your life. Get here asap. I told my mom I was moving, and I was gone the next day.

The devil will try anything to get you to abort your destiny. Do not fall for it. I do not know what made that spirit think I would kill myself because he was dead. I was glad my abuse ended. How it ended was out of my hands. I would pray every night for it to end. Why in the world would I kill myself to join him! That was straight from hell. And no, thank you. Yes, I will admit, I ran amok.

Before I really understood the power and control the past has on a person, I did some things, that when I look back, were wrong. Now, I should have known better, but, when all you know is abuse, the abused often become the abuser.

I had multiple boyfriends and did not really care. There was one who I finally gave my heart to. Unbeknownst to me. I did not know I was in love with him until we parted ways. I had to go back to New York to help my mom with her medical issues, which I can say worked out well. During that time, we had talked about the past and I saw her from a different light.

Nugget zone*

Take time to reflect on the feelings of others when appropriate. I thought I knew everything, but when the true owner of the emotions shares their thoughts, ideas, or intentions then, you will know the truth.

I began to learn more about the faith and fear my mother had in her life at that moment. She was afraid to reach out to anyone for help and did not know who she could trust. Unfortunately, these things happen to adults as well as children and often simultaneously in these types of situations. Please be on the lookout for any clues or signs that seem wrong. It is better to speak to someone you can trust than to have something happen and live with it on your conscience.

Back to the story. I got involved with a nice friend, which, I respect for whom he has become. Out of that relationship, I had given birth to a beautiful daughter before getting married. It was hard. Again, I prayed and asked God to help me with her, and I gifted her back to God. I was mindful to live a settled life with her. I did not want her to grow up moving from place to place. But I will tell you, we did move several times, around five times to be exact. Always to a better life and to make sure she was well taken care of.

Finally, when I got my mind and self together, it was 18 years later and my daughter was graduating high school. Because your children pick up your emotions and try to emulate and become the protector of your heart. That task does not belong to them. And we must teach them how to be healthy. Yes, single parents go through a lot, but so do married people. And when we realize the peace we are seeking does not come from our spouse, boyfriend, or significant other, we choose to be happy.

God is truly awesome! I went on to college. A few to be exact. The last university I attended was especially significant for me. I graduated from there with my doctorate after several attempts and life's circumstances happening. But, as I said, the most significant thing that happened there was my admission advisor and I was talking one day, and he began to speak this into my spirit (we never met physically): these are his words to me

"He said: you know, I see you standing before an audience doing like Joyce Meyer. He could not see my face, but my husband and I had been talking about speaking to other women, and men, helping them to get free from their past".

My husband and I looked at each other. Because my advisor and I were on the phone talking about school, we began talking about life in general. He told me he had a cat; I said I was a dog person myself, but when he started talking to me, the hairs on my arm started standing up and my husband just looked and nodded in agreement. Of course, we told him we were talking about that as well. Sometimes we look for the right reverend, overseer, or bishop to speak to us, and God is using ordinary people, those without titles, to speak to us.

We think they are the only ones who can speak to us, but I keep in my mind that when Saul was on the road to Damascus, the donkey stopped and talked to him. Not comparing the advisor to a donkey, but the point is if you are willing and obedient, you can hear from God regardless of the vessel. A requirement for grad school was to submit an essay about the journey on which we were embarking. What the advisor did not know was I had spoken to that scenario in the essay. Here you can say, God was reading my mail. It is just a saying to mean that God already knew what was happening before you or I thought it.

3
CHAPTER
Building A God Relationship

Mothers are the most loving, caring, and compassionate people but the most selfish, egotistical human beings. If you say not me, then girlfriend, look a little closer, especially you. In my scholarly venture, I was informed there are grey areas in literature. As a scholar, I differed in that opinion as well, but I learned to acquiesce my opinion to the scholars before me. However, as a single mom, it remained black or white where my child was concerned if he was not good enough to me after a brief conversation or complaint session, then we did not see each other anymore. You understand where I am coming from, ladies and gentlemen.

The one thing I would remember after the entire tear-stained conversation or little pieces of wisdom I did not share was this:

Nugget zone

When you complain and share your hurts with your bestie, you will get over it, but it will take some time for us because someone we love was hurt, and now we want to exact revenge. So, ladies, gents, and young folks, learn how to share and what to share because the other party is prejudiced and will seek reparation without your consent (sometimes). Outside of abuse, whether emotional, physical, or mental, learn maturity. This does not mean give him or her a free pass to ostracize and demean who you are. Be aware that when you share personal information, it will come back to bite that backside. It is the nature of humanoids/homo-sapiens, when feeling trapped caught by someone to cast the light on the other individual. Do not take it personal. Adam did it to Eve (although she was the inital contact). When God asked Adam what was up in the garden, (Genesis 3:12 read it for yourself) he played the aw-shucks blame game, see, it's nothing new, but when we recognize our part, we become humble and forgiving to be forgiven.

Parents, I am telling you this is not news to any of us. Our parents, bless their hearts, gave us as much as they could impart to us, but now we must release our children to grow up. Do you ever wonder why some of our children dislike being referred to as children when we speak of them? And we will argue with them, sometimes taking them down memory lane: I remember when you were such and such age, doing this or that, and now you are talking about being grown. And rightly so, take that young man or woman out of the sandbox or off those monkey bars and let them be.

Some of us did not care for when it was said to us and now, we are repeating it. I told my daughter I needed to grow up. The coddling our children can also bite them, and us, in the buttocks when it comes to letting go. Be mindful and with all your strength, cut the umbilical cord, or as the old folks say, cut that apron string and let go. The best thing we can do as parents is not dwarf our children. Paul puts it this way, stop procrastinating and let the child grow up. The reason, mom or dad, is because we are holding on to them. like life is going to end when they leave. Unless you are about to do something... it will not. Life will continue to move forward.

Nugget zone

Life never takes you backwards unless you go backwards, and you cannot really do that. All you can and will be is stuck. Now think about that.

Start living life. One of the most blessed gifts to provide in our family is to let them see what it takes to be in a meaningful relationship. Sometimes the child is trying to make sure you are not left alone. They do ponder what will happen if they leave. It is up to the parent to make sure that the child does not carry luggage it was not meant to carry.

Too often, parents put their children on a guilt trip about whatever the subject matter is at that moment. We laugh and say oh, I did not mean it, but you did. That child might not say anything at that time, but in their hearts, they contemplate what would you do or how will you make it without them.

Honestly, they become your parent. When you start playing with their emotions like that, they mimic those actions in their relationships. Think about it. Whenever you ask for something that will take away from their plans, they must adjust, if they do not say no. Heaven forbid if they say no, some may go in on them like an enema. I did this and that for you. Guess what, baby, you were supposed to. That was your charge as a parent. Do not guilt them into doing anything for you.

When we do things like that, we stunt their growth as adults. We also limit our ability to be the man or woman God has destined for us to be. Just because the child is leaving the home, does not mean they will not visit. But if you act like they are supposed to wait on you hand and foot, they may not come back once they leave. Their relationships will mirror what you have done to them.

That is the time to go after what you put on hold to raise them. Do not cramp your style. If you find someone who they dislike, guess what, they will get over it. They may find someone who you do not care for. Guess what, if you do not like the person, keep your mouth shut. Pray.

Think about when you were having your fling. Someone in your family probably did not care for the person you brought to the family cookout or reunion. Instead of voicing your opinion around the entire family, take them to the side if you must and speak to them. Do it in love and not out of jealousy or animosity.

We are always teaching our family to grow, accept, and learn that it is not always my way or the highway. Grow up and reclaim your life, vitality, and peace. Make wise choices moving forward, weigh out the actions. Your actions (count the cost). Develop an open relationship with your children, so they can or want to come and share whatever is going on in their lives. The only way that can happen is if you show them you are mature enough to handle your own business.

Let us face it folks, we are all subject to attitudes, immature moments, and so forth. So, if you are going to discuss your past, please, please, please, pray! Shall I give you a page long of *please?* Lol. Make note that because you share, the other party does not have to. No one is obligated to do so.

Sometimes in our zealousness to open up, be transparent, or any other words you choose to fill the reason why you discussed your past, remember it is something you felt to do; not everyone believes the same way. That is why we are not clones. And remember, ladies and gents, opening that door does not secure your position or place in the heart or eyes, or yes, I did go there (the bed). The decision you make is yours to live with. Unfortunately, sometimes sharing can be the Achilles heel.

Boy, if we honestly look back over those moments using the wisdom we have gained, we could say we got played. Frankly, we let our pride and honey-dripping, lovesick emotions take us to a place some of us knew or know better. This is not to say, we would have at that moment done things different, if our inner self was hollering, run Forest! (Forest Gump); but we succumb to our libidio and syrup dripping, mind-twirling words and ran out the door. Ha, if we could have done so, maybe our names would have been Joseph or Josephette

In keeping things real, we were naïve and used the excuse, I love … If we loved ourselves just a little bit more or had been told more often, just maybe we could have withstood the moment. But do not despair. There is hope.

One wise person said that is the reason pencils have erasers on the end. If it were that simple, however, using the intelligence and scholarly knowledge ascertained over the decades, we could obtain peace. You do not have to hang your head in despair. Instead of saying yes, wait. If you were told if you love me, you would. Do not be beguiled by your lust. You will lose your peace. The only person you would be hurting is yourself. Did you really want to do it, or did it because you thought you would win brownie points? Before it sounds like I am bitter, I will answer that with a resounding no! at the time of my tête-à-tête,I honestly did not have nor was I seeking a relationship. Because I was being phony with my true self, I entered a life-altering relationship, which I never intended to happen at that time." But, I would not change it for the world.

So, take it from someone who has been there, got the tee shirt, and has now shredded that bad boy; be true to yourself. Playing games, pulling punches, and then crying wolf does not wear well on males or females. Too often we do not speak up for fear of hurting someone's feelings. Let us not sell the other person short; they will get over you. To whom are we lying? Them or yourself? But what you lost can only be replaced after time and learning to forgive yourself. Getting your peace back will take arduous work and dedication to being you.

To find a life partner, you must know your self-worth. No one can give it to you or tell you this. It is within you. If you do not know this, refer to the beginning of the chapter or book if you must, or better yet sit the book down and make a list of your Pros& Cons. What you will do versus what you will not do. And if you have a grey area, as the scholars say, find it and work on it. Realize when you are at your best, making positive changes and clear decisions, you will find peace when asked why. Someone will notice those things and gravitate to you because you are being authentic.

Now, remember you have grown past being momma or daddy and are ready for a mature relationship with others. Even if you are still waiting for your Mr. Right or Boaz; today you read of females saying they are waiting on their Boaz. Sister, let me please, read the scripture on the preparation Ruth went through before she met him. Make sure you are content in being you.

Do not treat that person like you gave birth to them. They are not in the market for parents, if so, be alone; (run, Forest) that relationship will be an emotional weight, and peace will elude you.

Free yourself from those around you, gave birth to, and learn to live in peace with yourself. Do not get caught playing Wendy to Peter Pan", and men, do not get caught playing daddy to a grown woman (unless it's role-playing night).

Be an adult about your life and peace up. Maturing and aging are a fact of life. Just find someone to share those moments with that you can enjoy without reverting to a mother hen or rooster. You will find your best living when you find your peace. You will always have your past; do not let it have you. Move forward and forget those things. You will never see the beauty in front of you if you keep looking back. It will fade with time. Do not fall into being gullible or credulous when told if you love me, you will do this.

Guess what, if you loved me, you would not have made such a statement. I will inject a little story here about how I met my husband.

The first time I saw my husband, I did not like him. I did not think twice about anything concerning him. I was the pastor's armorbearer at the church. And may I just say, the best of them. There was a team of us working to secure the well-being of the pastor and his wife at every service. The role of the armor bearer was to be the first at the church and the last to leave.

I was also a single mother at the time, so that meant a lot of sacrifices came with the position. There was no time for anything else, as far as I knew. Getting to the church at 6 a.m. on Sundays, and taking public transportation was no easy feat. Getting my daughter up and out of the house to catch the bus posed challenges at times, but we did it. However, one Sunday after service, the pastor had me relay a message about meeting him after service. I just walked up to him and said, the pastor wants to speak to you and walked away. He followed me to the pastor's office, and that was it.

Sometime later, he began coming to the ministry on a frequent basis. I still did not pay attention to him because my focus was on ministry, my daughter, and singing. We did not hold conversations other than hello and the pleasantries that come with being nice. He soon began traveling with us to other ministries, and my daughter got a break. Every time someone saw us together, they would say we looked like a nice couple. And like children, we were not us. We just served in the ministry together.

Finally, one day I remember calling him because I was traveling back and forth to North Carolina from Virginia. I was talking to my daughter and asked her did she think he liked me? And she said yes. A blind man can see that, and she laughed. I was at the tire shop and decided to call him and asked did he like me. Well, he said yeah, you got a problem with that? I was floored. I hung up the phone and did not speak to him after that.

Until 2005. A few months passed between the last time we spoke.

My daughter and I were in North Carolina looking for a new place when my oldest sister died. The pastor, his wife, cousin, and hubby were already living in North Carolina. The pastor asked him to drive us back to Virginia to meet up with my sister to go to New York. My daughter and I were staying at an extended stay in NC while I looked for an apartment for us. When he picked me up, he said to me one day I am going to take you out and give you roses. Fast forward, summertime came, and he helped move my daughter and me down to North Carolina. We still did not connect because he was working on himself and a relationship, ha ha. It was about two to three years before we started dating.

Well, it was my daughter's sixteenth birthday, and we went to the store to pick up her cake for the party. A couple saw us and said you guys look great together. How long have you been married? We looked at each other and laughed. Maybe this is where God began to set us up. We did not make any gestures toward each other, so where was all this coming from?

We would get that question in many of the places we visited whether church or socially with the pastor and wife. I started deferring the response to him because I would excuse myself. We were still platonic because I was not looking for anyone, thing, or body. I was focusing on nothing. See, the truth was, I was running from being involved or loving anyone else besides my daughter and God. Some people think that is how life is supposed to be. But God said He came that we may enjoy life to its full and in abundance. Hiding does not provide that. Another scare tactic from within. It still took me several months before I spoke to my husband after all he did to show me he cared.

Long story short, I was in prayer the night before, and the Lord asked me how long are you going to push him away. My response was that he was already dating, and I was an intercessor for the ministry. This prayer time is about the ministry, not him. And God said, yes, it is. I said OKAY. What do I need to pray about? After I finished praying, it was time for church.

That morning on the way to service, I asked him what was going on in his life. We never discussed anything about our private lives with each other. It was a silent ride. For thirty-five minutes. I finally broke and told him, I do not like praying all night long for people who do not listen to God. He was shocked. When we arrived at the service, he left prayer early and I told him if you are not back by 5 p.m. I know you did not do what God said. He was at my house at 4:55 p.m. with five minutes to spare.

Then we put all our cards on the table with each other. All the clothes from the closet were hanging out. In other words, we held nothing back when we started sharing our past. It took some time, and we knew we both needed healing from past relationships. The good and bad ones because of soul ties that were created. We worked through them slowly and are still working on them. Even now.

A few months later, we finally started officially dating. When we told the pastor, his wife had the nerve to say, it's about time. We looked at each other with that stupid look as if to say, huh? Well, fourteen years later I can honestly say, when hubby says he is going to do something, he does. Through all our disappointments and heartaches, God did not let us down.

I have mentioned it before, and I think it is worth repeating, God does not let us down. We may feel God is a little slow answering our prayers, but rest assure you will receive an answer. I remember mentioning to my husband one time about prayer. As a habit, we always want things done yesterday. However, we also fail to realize people have free will. They make their choices based upon how they feel. We can want things done as the words come out of our mouths, but we are not responsible for what other people do with the request.

For example, I never grew up thinking anything as horrendous as abuse would happen to me. Nor was I aware things of such nature existed. That was in my little world or sphere of existence, rainbows, white puppies, and candy. Did God know? Yes. When I look in the scripture where He told Moses to tell Pharaoh to release His people, did He know it would not happen? Of course. Did that stop Moses from making the request? No. But, God knew exactly what was going to happen, and just like He knew then, He still knows the outcome. Like Moses and the others, we must trust the process.

Do bad things still happen in life? Yes! Why? Because of choices or, as some say, freewill.

Pharaoh and everyone else have the same opportunity to make decisions, good or bad. We ask things of others when we know the answers before asking. Does it stop us? Everyone could do good or evil. The consequences or results from the action will still come.

My husband has a saying that I believe is worth mentioning: Choice is a wonderful thing to have, if you use it right. As Uncle Ben said in Spiderman: "with great power comes great responsibility."

4
CHAPTER

Transparency in God's Time

Today, there are people who have been through so many things that wreak havoc on their lives. I considered the need to be transparent of high importance when dealing with the ills of society and getting free from personal scars. Will it hurt? Yes, of course it will. However, when the healing begins, you will know what you are being healed from.

Trauma attacks every living thing. Human beings are not the only existing ones who undergo trauma. Trauma is defined as a deeply distressing or disturbing experience. Your traumatic experience may not be as extensive as others;nonetheless it has already or may continue to define your life and energy.

When you have experienced something that continues to impact the very essence of your being, it was traumatic. The best thing for us to do is to pull the cover off at your own pace. And recognize the role it plays in formulating decisions. I can assure you; it has impacted my life to the point that I almost turned my back on the very one who was designed by God to help me heal. As I continued to search for peace, I came across a few suggested readings by the ministry I was a part of at the time: *Hung by the tongue*, by Francis P. Martin; Comfort For the Wounded Spirit by Frank and Ida Mae Hammond, and Sit,Walk,Stand by Watchman Nee. Those books have and continue to impact my life and how I pursue things.

We sometimes think no one has ever been through what I am going through. And the truth is, there is someone who can speak to the pain, turmoil, and emotions you are experiencing. I am not an advocate of telling children about past or history outside of medical. However, you can discuss the past when they are mature enough to handle it. Pray before you do. It can be damaging to their psyche or more confusing, leading you down a road that you never intended or dealt with yourself.

See, some people feel the need to clear their conscience when they are about to check out of existence. They must speak in that scenario, be an adult and talk to the person before it is too late to get clarification. On the other side of the coin, your children could learn something and become callous towards the individuals, when you have been delivered or made peace with the situation and your past.

I recall experiencing both sides of this scenario. Sometimes people use this to their advantage to hurt and drive a wedge between family members. As twisted as it may sound, both ways can bring up the subject matter that can eventually have you reconcile your heart to obtain peace. You can take the sting away from the enemy by facing it head-on and talking about it.

Have you ever had a person come to you to tell you something that was supposed to be a secret, or they begin the conversation asking did you know such and such? Please get away from that person, just like the devil trying to throw a curve ball at you. He walks about, seeking people he can devour. You do not have to the one.

There are ways to keep your peace and defeat the enemy. Keep your environment clear of nonsense and chatter that destroy peace. Stop the conversation before it starts and ask if we can get that person to join us. Most often than not, they will say I was just trying to tell you something. Is that something worth the peace you would be giving up from that grey knowledge?

Revel in the good times that were. Maybe they were few and far between, as the old folks would say, but they were there. Do not discount your history because of the issues you endured. They are what made you strong enough to continue facing life. And for those who say they cannot go on, seek professional help. It can get dark, no lie, but the refreshing part is to know that the next day will come, and you can and will win with the grace of God, family, and friends. I wanted to and did hate him for years. And wished, prayed, and cried and told God he did not love me. He was not real because of everything I was going through. If you were, you would save me from this horrible life.

The Spirit of God told me, if I did not love you, my only son would not have died for you. Then I would discuss my abuser, and He said I died for him too. I said did I knew what kind of person he was. He said, my son died for everyone. I know what he would do, but he had to be given a chance just like you. I am a just God, my son hung on the cross for many who would deny Him, but He did it anyway.

Wow, so when I think or pray, I say thank you lord for saving me. For loving me so much that you gave your son for me. I appreciate it very much. Sometimes we get so caught up in me, we cannot see God working it out.

As I close this book, I will let you know these things. Remember when I said my mom wrote a letter saying if she died first, it was because of the chaos and destruction caused by our abuser Well, mom did not. She lived to see my child born and become a beautiful young lady.

The best part about this life I am living now is, not only was I totally restored to God, but my mom gave her life to Christ at a service where the son was the pastor of the church. HA!! Take that devil! You even lost the soul of someone who hated God because of their disdain for preachers. You have got to be shouting out of your shoes now. The enemy thought he had the family going down the tube with him, and everyone is now living their life for God. It is awesome when you recognize the route is not as important as the goal.

There are many things that will deter you from being the best that you are meant to be. No one has a monopoly in the pain market. Whatever has hindered you, let it go. Find things that will bring you joy. Laughter is like a medicine. And because it does the heart good to rejoice.

Find something that will overshadow the pain in a positive way and think on those things. It will do wonders for your everyday attitude and make you a more enjoyable person to be around. You have more to share in life than your pain. Someone is counting on you, looking at you for answers to their problems. This does not mean you have the answers. Adjust your focus and consider your experiences. We all have them, but it does not dictate our future.

King James Version

"Philippians 4:8:

Finally, brethren, whatsoever things are true, whatsoever things are just, whatsoever things are pure, whatsoever things are lovely, whatsoever things are of good report; if there be any virtue, and if there be any praise, think on these things."

I know throughout this brief book, many of you wondered how your story will end. Is what I have been through worth writing or telling someone about it? Well, the truth is, you will be given a myriad of answers from well-wishers to unsolicited critics, but what did God say? Your final answer does not come from a list of people who sit around and discuss what you said and how they would have done things. The reason you decided to write or put pen to paper is because it heals in time the things you thought you never would get closure from.

Many times, we sit and think what would someone else do, and the fact of the matter is this... do you honestly think they would or could be as forthright with the past or present as you? I am not putting medals on anyone, not even myself, for that matter. As I sit and write this book, there have been many nights I thought about not sharing because I did not want anyone to know or kick the sleeping dog. But if I am not willing to show how the grace of God kept me and what He can do if we allow Him to, then I am no better than those who complain and sit in the same spot year after year.

Remember the lepers that were healed by Jesus? There were ten of them, right? But only one returned to thank Him (Luke 17:11-19). Although all of them were healed, only one received complete wholeness. I say that to tell you, everyone who reads, listens, or you converse with, will not be grateful for what you have imparted into their lives. You may never know, or there could be the one, who returns to you and says, thank you. You have helped me overcome or given me the courage to say something to my family.

I can honestly say it will not be easy and some may dispute what you have to say, but the real test is do you trust God and believe He will give you His peace to overcome the naysayers? If we did only those things which pleased others, how would you feel? They will never be pleased with you. Will you stop trying to please them and please God? The maker of mankind? When you take your final rest, do you want to hear well done or depart?

The peace we receive from knowing God is our source and a present help and is plenty strong enough to get through this life. Knowing and accepting God as our source is sufficient for anything we must face. Knowing that He is just a call, prayer, or shout away to me is awesome.

You have been called to be greater than your past. It is history, and those things are always going to be behind you. They are in your rearview mirror for a reason. You are moving away from them to get to your expected end. Do not give up in the middle of the road. There is too much life left to enjoy, share, and experience. Find your peace and live life to the fullest. The blank pages that will follow are for you to write your ideas, feelings, and focus on your future. Please remember or write Post-it-Notes and place them where you will see them daily. To move beyond where you are now, you must speak what God says about you. Whether you feel like you have reached that pinnacle or not. Why? Because your thoughts will impact your life. Why speak negativity into your future. Those seeds will bring a harvest. What will you sow?

REFERENCES

Amplified Version King James

Bacharach, Burt (composer,1985) "Finders of Lost Love", Performed by Jones, Glenn & Warwick, Dionne

Forrest Gump movie (1994, July 6), Director: Robert Zemeckis; Screenplay by Eric Roth

Holy Bible

Hammond, Frank & Ida Mae (1992) *Comfort for the Wounded Spirit*

King James Version

Martin, P. Francis (1972) *Hung by the Tongue*

Nee, Watchman (1977) *Sit, Walk, Stand*

Printed in the United States
by Baker & Taylor Publisher Services